IMAGES
of America

MILLS COUNTY

This map of Mills County was made out of apples for a Glenwood Apple Carnival. In 1897, the *Trans-Mississippian* magazine called Mills County the "banner fruit county of the Western continent" with apples that had won first honors at the 1876 Philadelphia Exposition and the 1893 Chicago World's Fair. (Courtesy of the Mills County Historical Society.)

ON THE COVER: This was the footbridge across Keg Creek between Vine Street and the Iowa Institution for Feeble-Minded Children (IIFMC) in Glenwood. In 1893, the *Mills County Tribune* newspaper promised that the creek offered an "oozy and slimy but delicious paddle." The footbridge washed away in 1912. (Courtesy of the Mills County Historical Society.)

IMAGES
of America

MILLS COUNTY

Ryan Roenfeld

ARCADIA
PUBLISHING

Published by Arcadia Publishing
Charleston SC, Chicago IL, Portsmouth NH, San Francisco CA

Library of Congress Control Number: 2009936025

For all general information contact Arcadia Publishing at:
Telephone 843-853-2070
Fax 843-853-0044
E-mail sales@arcadiapublishing.com
For customer service and orders:
Toll-Free 1-888-313-2665

Visit us on the Internet at www.arcadiapublishing.com

To my children Savannah, Connor, and John

CONTENTS

ACKNOWLEDGMENTS

The author would like to thank Carrie Merritt and the dedicated volunteers of the Mills County Historical Society who have helped keep the county's history alive for future generations. Without their encouragement and assistance this project would have never materialized. Likewise, the author appreciates the assistance and contributions of Denise Crawford and Jackie Harless at the Glenwood Public Library, Rachel Carlile, Gary Roenfeld, Richard Lincoln, Erin Lenz, Dr. Richard Warner, Wanda Ewalt, and the offices of the Mills County Soil and Water Conservation District. Lastly, the author would like to thank his editor, Ted Gerstle, along with Amanda Pokorski, Savannah Pokorski, and Connor Hinshaw for their patience during the completion of this book. All photographs are courtesy of the Mills County Historical Society unless otherwise noted.

INTRODUCTION

The history of Mills County stretches back well before 1714, when Etienne Bourgmont made his way up the Missouri River to become the first known European to reach the mouth of the Platte River. The Hill archeological site on Pony Creek was dated at 5300 B.C., and the Glenwood culture of the Central Plains tradition established a horticultural society after 1050 A.D. that continued for the next 300 years.

The area was included as part of French Louisiana in 1682 and then Spanish Louisiana after 1764. European interest increased after 1739 when the Mallet brothers traveled west along the Platte River to reach Santa Fe, which stimulated the fur trade west to the Pawnee villages and the Rocky Mountains. The Point aux Poules in what is now St. Marys Township and Bellevue, Nebraska, across the river became important transit points to St. Louis. In the southwestern portion of the county on the Missouri River were the Île aux Cinq Barils. The nearby muddy stream was anglicized to Five-Barrel Creek and is now Keg Creek. The land on both sides of the Missouri River from the Nemaha River north to the Boyer River was considered Otoe territory when Lewis and Clark stopped in 1804 in the vicinity of present day Applewood Road. In 1811, Henry Brackenridge reported that crossing the mouth of the Platte River was "regarded by the navigators of the Missouri as a point of as much importance, as the equinoctial line amongst mariners. All those who had not passed it before, were required to be shaved, unless they could compromise the matter by a treat."

Samuel Allis arrived in 1834 as part of a Presbyterian mission to the Pawnee and later settled in St. Marys Township as a government interpreter. In 1837, the Potawatomi Reserve was established with a subagency located in what is now Platteville Township. Approximately 2,000 Potawatomi, Ottawa, and Chippewa from Illinois and Wisconsin spread out across southwest Iowa. Wabansi, Half-Day, Joseph LaFramboise, and Perish Le Clere all lived in what is now Mills County. The first subagent was Edwin James who described the "Missouri Bottom . . . everywhere low and contains many lagoons and low swampy parts" where "improvements made . . . will be very liable to be washed away by changes in the course of the stream." The Loess Hills were "sharp broken and rather sterile knobs . . . wholly destitute of arable land or timber of any value except for fuel." To the east stretched "many tracts of fine soil sufficiently smooth and level for cultivation, but there is in general a great want of timber for the purposes of permanent settlement."

Changes came fast after 1844, when subagency blacksmith Elisha Stephens quit to lead the first wagon train west through the Sierra Nevada Mountains into California. That year Henry Carleton found the line between the reservation and Missouri dotted with whiskey traders who sold on easy credit, including Rufus Hitchcock who sued Wabonsi in 1846 for unpaid debts. That same year the Potawatomi agreed to move to Kansas, Iowa became a state, and the Mormons began to arrive at the Missouri River after they were forced from Nauvoo, Illinois. Kanesville was the largest town they established as the seat of both religion and government after Pottawattamie County was created in 1848. That year Lebbeus Coons was named Bishop of the Lower Area. Coons had three wives and lived at what is now Vine and Tyson Streets in Glenwood.

Thaddeus Culbertson passed through in 1850 and found "little log cabins with their big fireplaces, big air holes and the old rifle over the door, or the mantel piece." Culbertson traveled "along the bottom and through the timberland of the Missouri and it has been as bad as I want to see." The Mormon *Frontier Guardian* newspaper described the "Coonville precinct," named after Lebbeus Coons, where Coolidge's "good gristmill, and excellent sawmill" were in operation and there was "plenty of good timber, fine prairie, and excellent water." Agents for the newspaper in 1850 included Joseph Pendleton at St. Francis, Jonathon Browning at Brownings, Christian Clapper in Old Agency, Joseph Coolidge at Coolidge's Mill, and David Dixon at Bethlehem City.

These new communities also attracted "mobocrats," in the words of Coonville resident Silas Hillman, and a few opportunists. In 1850, Col. Joseph Sharp came to Coonville to open a law practice. The 1918 *History of Nebraska* described Sharp as "a man of italic individuality" whose features had been "scarred, indented, and pitted with smallpox. That dreadful disease had bleared, glazed over, and destroyed the sight of his left eye, and at the same time had twisted and deeply indented his prominent nose, which looked somewhat awry; so that, altogether, the victim's facial expression was rather repellant."

In 1851, the Iowa legislature divided Pottawattamie County into 29 much smaller counties independent of officials in Kanesville. One of them was named after Frederick Mills, a lawyer and major in the recent war with Mexico who disappeared during the Battle of Cherubsco. A post office opened in Coonville, which became the county seat when Mills County was organized by Sheriff Noyes in August 1851.

Mormon bishop Libbeus Coons was elected the county's first prosecuting attorney, and a wood courthouse was built on what is now Locust Street in Glenwood. The 1881 *History of Mills County* reported that the Mormons were soon subject to the "denial of the right of suffrage" and then "disallowing the privilege to sit on juries." When the first session of district court opened that fall the judge was James Sloan, an Irish immigrant who the 1881 History pronounced "illiterate, though prompt and decisive in rendering his judgments." A mob gathered at the courthouse on Locust Street, refused to let him inside, and then followed him into Coolidge's store where Judge Sloan convened the court, immediately adjourned, and left town.

Daniel Solomon later wrote that these disputes grew "into contentions and feuds of first a personal and local character, then into clans" with "fears on one side and threats on the other." Colonel Sharp tried to play the middle and was trusted by no one, and what is now Locust Street in Glenwood was "constantly filled with people and scenes of strife and anger occurred almost daily."

In late 1851, Brigham Young called for the Mormons to leave for Salt Lake City as they began to leave the homes and farms established over the past five years. District court resumed at Glenwood in 1852 under Judge Bradford, who the 1881 county history recalled would "go to church, to court, or around amongst friends" while "half shaven, one foot slip shod, and otherwise slatternly attired." Sharp was prosecuting attorney, and at that year's election, Hiram Bennett became county judge as the first non-Mormon elected to office. At the same time, Sharp was elected the representative of 29 almost unpopulated counties in western Iowa. By the end of 1852, a notice appeared in the Mormon *Frontier Guardian* about two stores and two hotels at "Glenwood." In January 1853, the Iowa legislature recognized Glenwood as the official seat of Mills County, while Sharp, Judge Bennett, John Sivers, and Oliver Tyson divided up Coonville and renamed the streets.

The 1852 census found 1,463 people in Mills County, and the first records from 1853 show West Liberty, Plattville, Rawles, Council Bluffs, and Silver Creek Townships. Kanesville became Council Bluffs after most of the Mormons left although about 2,000 remained behind spread across southwest Iowa.

In late 1853, a mass meeting at Glenwood enthusiastically promoted the organization of Nebraska Territory. In February 1854 Judge Bennett, Peter Sarpy, and William English established what is now Bellevue, Nebraska, and the new territory was created by Congress three months later. The first territorial legislature convened in Omaha with several Mills County residents in attendance, including Sharp, who was named president of the territorial council and Judge Bennett, who was president pro tem of the Nebraska House. The effort by Glenwood residents to get Plattsmouth designated the territorial capital was flustered by Sharp, whom no one trusted, and two Glenwood attorneys who switched their vote in exchange for bribes in Omaha city lots. Sorensen's 1876 *History of Nebraska* noted an "indignation" meeting was held in Glenwood against "their representatives for misrepresenting them in the Nebraska legislature." One of them barely escaped a public whipping and the other died soon afterwards although Sorensen noted "whether he died from grief at the indignation of Glenwood, or not, this historian has not been able to ascertain."

By 1856 Mills County's population had doubled to 3,102. In 1892, the *Mills County Tribune* noted that the earliest residents "settled in the timber, and avoided as much as possible coming into possession of any large tracts of prairie lands." Judge Bennett left for Colorado, and Judge Tyson sold the county's swamplands to build a new courthouse in Glenwood. Everything came by way of steamboats from St. Louis, but in 1858, the Council Bluffs and St. Joseph railroad was organized to build south from Council Bluffs along the Missouri River.

Mills County elected L.W. Tubbs in 1858 as the last of the old-style county judges. Tubbs had left New York during the Gold Rush and served in the first California legislature before he came to Mills County in 1856. The route of the Burlington and Missouri River Railroad west to the Missouri river became a source of dispute, and a railroad agent named McClary reported in 1860 that Mills County was the "toughest country I ever got in both in living and inhabitants."

With the outbreak of the Civil War in 1861, William English raised Company A of the Fourth Iowa Infantry at the courthouse, Judge Tubbs organized the Mills County Minute Men militia, and a vigilance committee was created. In 1863, Joe Fallon decided to use the American flag flying above the courthouse for target practice and was beat to the ground with the crutch of one-legged James Nelson. A mass meeting was held where Fallon was forced to kneel, take an oath, pay a hefty fine, and get out of town for good. In May 1865, the vigilance committee hung James Henderson, who the Glenwood *Opinion* newspaper called a "saloon keeper, gambler and loafer" prone to "treasonable sentiments." Two years later, the vigilance committee dragged Henderson's two brothers-in-law, William and Patrick Lawn, out of a Council Bluffs hotel and hung them.

The Council Bluffs and St. Joseph Railroad was running two trains a day from Council Bluffs south through Mills County in 1868, and a new county jail was built on the east side of Glenwood's Courthouse Square. In late 1869, the Burlington Railroad was completed west to the Missouri River, and several new towns sprang into existence within just a few weeks. Ten years later the *Mills County Republican* newspaper reported that a "gang of 76 men are laying track" for the Council Bluffs and St. Louis Railroad at the "rate of one mile per day." This further stimulated the honorable western pastime of town site speculation, while the Burlington Railroad built branch lines and a bridge west across the Missouri River.

In 1880, county residents grew upset that their taxes had paved the streets of Glenwood around the courthouse and presented a petition to the county board to move the courthouse to Malvern. In just 13 years Malvern had grown to over 1,000 people by 1882, with three railroads in town by 1890, after the Tabor and Northern Railroad was built and the Council Bluffs and St. Louis Railroad became part of the Wabash and Pacific Railroad. By 1895, Mills County had grown to 15,187 people, including 36 "colored" and 1,227 foreign-born. More than half of the immigrants came from Germany with the rest from England, Sweden, Ireland, and elsewhere.

There were 1,741 farms in Mills County in 1905 that covered 255,410 acres. The county also had over 38,000 cattle, 61,000 swine, and 166,500 chickens. Another courthouse feud erupted between Glenwood and Malvern in 1906. Bribery was reported and someone stole the newspaper type from a Malvern newspaper just so that its charges against Glenwood could be answered the same day by the Glenwood *Opinion*. The lack of support from Malvern ended attempts to build a new courthouse in 1908, and it wasn't until 1959 that a new courthouse would be dedicated at Glenwood. An automobile bridge across the Missouri River to Plattsmouth, Nebraska, opened in the 1930s, and in 1952, the Bellevue Bridge opened.

The population of Mills County was just over 11,800 in 1971 with 4,400 people in Glenwood. That year the Burlington Northern Railroad was formed as branch lines were trimmed back and passenger service came to an end. Interstate 29 and the U.S. Highway 34 bypass around Glenwood were both constructed, and the Davies clock tower was dedicated on the courthouse lawn in Glenwood in 1974. The Burlington Northern Santa Fe railroad was created after a 1995 merger and continues to cross Mills County, where the 2000 census found 14,500 residents.

One

St. Marys and Oak Townships

Until 1857 Saint Marys and Oak Townships were combined as Council Bluffs Township with a population "mostly French, half breeds and Indians," according to Peter Hanson in 1846. A Missouri River ferry had operated there since 1830, and Peter Sarpy was the representative for the American Fur Company. The Nebraska post office opened during the California Gold Rush, which became Council Bluffs in 1850 and then Traders Point in 1853 after most of it was washed into the river.

Sarpy moved downriver to establish St. Marys where the Iowa House Hotel and Cerro Gordo Post Office opened in 1853. W. H. Taft described St. Marys at its peak as having two hotels, stores, a Catholic chapel, and several windmills, including gristmills and others for "making shingles and running machinery of various kinds." The first Nebraska newspaper was printed there in 1854, and in 1859, Lewis Morgan accompanied "three Frenchmen" to visit Samuel Allis, one of whom had "a Brule Dakota wife at St. Marys two miles below."

The Plumer Settlement appeared east in the hills after Heinreich Saar and Johann Plumer settled near the intersection of the roads between Coonville and Kanesville, and between Traders Point and Fort Des Moines. The area attracted waves of German immigrants who founded St. Bonefatzins Catholic and Salem Evangelical Lutheran Churches in the 1860s and the German Independent Church of Christ of Pony Creek Valley in 1897. The Missouri River washed away St. Marys, which was located south of Allis Road and west of 182nd Street.

The 1879 construction of the Council Bluffs & St. Louis Railroad created Lewis City. The village was soon renamed, and in early 1882, the *Mills County Journal* newspaper reported that "Minneola" contained two hotels, a lumberyard, brick yard, three "general merchandise houses," a blacksmith, two boot and shoe stores, a feed stable, and four saloons.

Down on the Missouri River was Hobo Island where up to 60 families lived in the 1890s raising corn and watermelon. The *Mills County Tribune* called their homes "pretty poor concerns" with dirt floors and "some decidedly tough looking people over there." The 1895 census listed 245 people in St. Marys Township and 1,265 in Oak.

This sketch was drawn by Swiss artist Rudolph Kurz in 1851 of what he called Council Bluffs where he found a "number of counterfeiters and gamblers." This was also known as Point aux Poules, Louse Point, St. Francisville, and Traders Point and played an important role in the Rocky Mountain fur trade after the 1790s. In 1850, Byron McKinstry passed through and found "plenty of Indians" along with "5 or 6 stores, 3 taverns, and 15 or 20 houses," which were all swept away by the floods of 1852.

This was confidence man Ben Marks's cabin at his Elk Grove Ranch in St. Marys Township in 1930. According to David Maurer, Marks was instrumental in developing the "Big Store" confidence game. Suckers from across the country were roped here where they bet on fake races and boxing and wrestling matches in what the Washington Post called the "biggest swindle on record." Federal authorities indicted 84 gang members in 1909, although Ben Marks was ultimately found innocent.

This was the barn on the Heinrich and Anna Timmermann farm in the West Liberty neighborhood. The Timmermanns immigrated from Germany in the 1880s and a decade later moved here, where they had an orchard and a truck garden and raised tomatoes for the Glenwood Canning Company. (Courtesy of Rachel Carlile.)

The first hotel in Mineola was built by Detlef Dohse at Fourth and Main Streets and was later sold to brothers Gus and "Peg-leg" Thompson. It was then run by the Huebner family before it was torn down in 1911. (Courtesy of Brenda Bichel Lewis.)

The Mineola Mercantile Company at Fourth and Main Streets was started by Michael Flammant, an immigrant from Luxembourg, who arrived in town in September 1879. In 1910, Ernest Hartje purchased a half interest in the store, and later Herman Peters became his partner. Peters had immigrated from Germany at the age of fifteen, bought Hartje out in 1914, and served as Mineola postmaster for 27 years. The photograph below shows Dewey and Martha Deitchler standing in front of the store in 1962 just before it was torn down. Martha Deitchler was Herman Peters's daughter. (Above courtesy of Brenda Bichel Lewis.)

This was the Mineola Frauen Verein in 1910. The group was organized by Pauline Flammant to help maintain the town cemetery. The organization's bylaws were rewritten from German into English in 1923, and it became known as the Mineola Women's Cemetery Association. (Courtesy of Brenda Bichel Lewis.)

This was Main Street in Mineola looking west toward Keg Creek around 1908. The brick building on the right housed the Mills County German Bank. When the bank was robbed in 1909, Fred Schoening asked temporary cashier Ferdinand Nipp if the men were trying to sell something, as he did not speak English. The bandits escaped into the cornfields east of town. (Courtesy of Brenda Bichel Lewis.)

The L. W. Bichel Opera House and Joe Deitchler's Pool Hall were built at Main and Fourth Streets in Mineola after a 1907 fire destroyed J. F. Bichel's General Store, the town hall, Deitchler's Barbershop and Pool Hall, and Claus Schroeder's Saloon. The opera house hosted a variety of entertainment along with a Sons of Hermann clubroom and a doctor's office upstairs. In 1915, these buildings were both destroyed by fire. Deitchler rebuilt his pool hall, which became the Palisades Ballroom after 1934 when Roy Wasserman took it over and attached a dance floor. The building was sold at a public auction in 1983 to establish a community center for the never incorporated community.

This was the view looking north on Fourth Street in Mineola toward the Wabash Railroad tracks around 1917. Across the street on the right can be seen the Bichel Brothers General Store on the former site of the opera house. The grain elevator built by Nipp and Kruse was at Fourth and Elm Streets, which early residents had dubbed Hog Street. On the left is the Danielson Hotel, which was owned by Jacob Piermann when it was demolished in 1921. (Courtesy of Brenda Bichel Lewis.)

This was the aftermath of a July 1928 wreck on the Wabash Railroad just outside Mineola after the 115-foot long trestle over Lone Tree Creek gave way during a heavy rain. Four crewmen and an unidentified hobo were killed when the two engines and six refrigerated meat cars plunged into the 40-foot gully. (Courtesy of Brenda Bichel Lewis.)

A Norfolk and Western train makes its way through Mineola in the 1960s. The Norfolk and Western Railroad leased the Wabash line southeast of Council Bluffs in 1960 and then absorbed it four years later. The rail line became part of the Colorado and Eastern Railroad in 1984, then the Iowa Southern Railroad, and was abandoned in 1988. It was then converted into the Wabash Trace, a 63-mile bicycle trail that stretches from Council Bluffs southeast to Missouri. (Courtesy of Brenda Bichel Lewis.)

The Spetman or Oak Bluff Number One country school in Oak Township was in the Loess Hills along what is now 196th Street south of Brohardt Avenue.

The Fourth grade class of Sand Hollow School in 1932 was made up of Roy Krabbenhoft, Pauline Schoening, and Glen Schoening, pictured here from left to right. Sand Hollow was located at present-day Dobney Avenue and 260th Street. (Courtesy of the Glenwood Public Library.)

Clarence Roenfeld, left, and his brother Elmer are seen here cutting grain in the 1930s. Keg Creek and Mineola can both be seen in the background. (Author's collection.)

From left to right are Albert Jens, Charlie Roenfeldt, Leo Jens, and unidentified. Albert worked as a farmhand and then married Charlotte Deitchler, served in World War I, and built a home near his parent's farm. (Courtesy of Genevieve Hunt.)

Seen here on their farm north of Mineola are Ferdinand (far right) and Alvena Deitchler (second from right) with two of their seven children, Linda (far left) and Charlotte (second from left). Linda later married Rudolph Miller, and Charlotte married Albert Jens. (Courtesy of Genevieve Hunt.)

This is a 1972 view looking north at the impound dam built on Pony Creek on the Raymond Anderson Farm. The 82-acre lake is administered by the Mills County Conservation Board, and a portion of the county park was listed on the National Register of Historic Places in 1971 due to the area's archeological significance. (Courtesy of the Mills County Soil and Water Conservation District.)

Two

PLATTEVILLE TOWNSHIP

Platteville Township contains several abandoned boom towns and ferry landings. Bethlehem City was established by the Mormons in 1850 near modern-day Karns Avenue and Kane Road. It became Sharpsburg by 1858 and then East Plattsmouth during the 1870s. California City appeared to the north in 1849 with city blocks set aside for potential churches, courthouses, and colleges, and the Florence Post Office briefly appeared. The P. T. Moss and Company store opened at Platteville by 1850, and Sam Martin applied for a ferry license the next year. The Andreas Nebraska history described Martin as "very profane, indulging in intoxicants to excess, and keeping an Otoe squaw who lived with him as his wife." In 1853, Martin became partners with Colonel Sharp in a log-trading house across the river. The Platteville Post Office opened in 1854, and that fall, Martin, Sharp, and some Glenwood businessmen gathered at the log-trading post to found what is now Plattsmouth, Nebraska.

Pacific City appeared in 1857 amidst speculation in western land and railroads. A post office opened and the town's plat covered 400 acres. Within a year, Pacific City had 90 houses, a hotel, church, schoolhouse, four stores, a steam sawmill, and a weekly newspaper. The Glenwood *Opinion* called the courthouse feud between Pacific City and Glenwood "one of the bitterest county seat wars in the history of the west" where "Brickbats, clubs and even pistols played a lively part." The Pikes Peak Rush to Colorado took many of its residents, and the post office briefly closed until it was reopened by William Vinton. It also achieved notoriety as the location of the illegal 1873 championship prizefight between Tom Allen and Ben Hogan. The town site was vacated in 1875, and the post office closed permanently in 1903.

Pacific Junction was first established in 1870 where the Council Bluffs and St. Joseph Railroad crossed the Burlington Railroad. The town was surveyed in 1871 and incorporated in 1882. In 1888, the *Malvern Leader* newspaper assured readers that "the hard characters" that gave Pacific Junction the "inevitable stigma that attaches to a new railroad town" were gone and "whiskey drinkers" had to "go to Plattsmouth or Glenwood." By 1895, there were 743 people in the township, and Pacific Junction had a population of 643 people.

The Burlington Railroad Bridge across the Missouri River to Nebraska was completed in 1880 and is shown here after the span was rebuilt in 1902. Previously the railroad used two steam ferries to transfer up to 200 train cars across the river every day. The narrow peninsula behind the bridge was the site of Sharpsburg or East Plattsmouth, which was surveyed in 1858 near the site of the Mormon ferry landing at Bethlehem and later became the Carolyn Wade Farm. (Author's collection.)

This was the Richardson's cable ferry, *Dollie Jane*, traveling across the Missouri river near where the Mormons had started the Bethlehem ferry in 1850. Peter Sarpy and Bill Kuhl later owned the ferry here. The *Paul Wilcox* steamboat ferry sank here in 1869, and in 1877, the *Mary McGee* steamboat ferry was sunk by ice chunks in the river. For a time in the 1890s, ferry service was provided for free by Plattsmouth merchants and John Richardson took over in 1910. Ferry service ended in 1930 after the opening of the Plattsmouth toll bridge.

The Missouri river steamboat *Arthur S.* pushes a sand sucker along in this October 1930 photograph while the natural gas pipeline was being laid underneath the river to Plattsmouth. Steamboats that sank in the Missouri River along the western edge of the county include the *Pirate* in 1842, the *Mary Cole* in 1856, the *General Grant* in 1866, and the 237-ton *W. W. Walker*, which was caught by a snag and went down in 1874.

Burlington Depot, Pacific Junction, Iowa.

This was the third depot constructed by the Burlington Railroad in Pacific Junction just south of Third Street and Iowa Avenue. President Cleveland spoke at the depot in 1887, as did President Roosevelt in 1936. A six-stall roundhouse was built in Pacific Junction in 1920, and in 1963, the Burlington Railroad moved its traffic control equipment here from Red Oak. For many years, the Burlington Refrigerator Express had a refrigerated boxcar facility in the community. (Courtesy of Gary Roenfeld.)

This was the Burlington Railroad yard at Pacific Junction where the rail lines converged running north to Council Bluffs, east to Chicago, south to Kansas City, and west across the Missouri River Bridge through Nebraska. By 1880, the three railroad lines at Pacific Junction were all consolidated into the Chicago, Burlington, and Quincy Railroad. Near the rail yard in Pacific Junction were a 40-acre stockyard, hobo jungles, and "seven drinking and pleasure houses," according to Morris Moore. (Courtesy of Richard Lincoln.)

The students above were attending the Pacific Junction High School around 1900, when Prof. William Moore oversaw the school. The photograph below shows the Pacific Junction School in 1908.

NO. 7   PUBLIC SCHOOL.   PACIFIC JCT. IOWA.

This was the K. P. Theatre Company's opera house in Pacific Junction. The 1918 businesses listed in the *Iowa State Gazetteer* included the opera company along with four general stores operated by the Anderson Brothers, Davis and Anderson Mercantile, John Olson and Son, and Hines and Company.

This was a blacksmith shop at Pacific Junction. The town had just over 500 residents by 1917, when Chris Gorn took over the blacksmith shop. Gorn was born in Council Bluffs to Danish immigrant parents, repaired steam engines to thresh local farms, and later opened a basket factory and sawmill on the southwest side of town. His brother George operated the theater in Pacific Junction, and in later years, Chris Gorn operated one of the town's gas stations. (Courtesy of Richard Lincoln.)

This was the Pacific Junction High School's football team in 1925. The graduating class the next spring included Lawrence Bogle, Elton Capps, Olaf Coffey, Opal Crossen, Cletus Edwards, Herbert Hansen, Bertha Lincoln, Ralph Lincoln, Katherine Moore, and Paul Lee. (Courtesy of Richard Lincoln.)

Otis "Cooney" Hopkinson stands in front of his barbershop on the south side of Lincoln Avenue in Pacific Junction. Businesses in Pacific Junction during the late 1930s included Boyle and Empkie's Hardware, Johnson's Meat Market, and Olson's General Store. (Courtesy of Richard Lincoln.)

From left to right, Lola Boquette, an unknown child, Myrna Harless, and Mrs. Harry Arnold stand on Lincoln Avenue in Pacific Junction during the 1947 flood. Lola came to Pacific Junction in 1930 after she married Howard Boquette. She served as the Justice of the Peace for 30 years, was an Avon representative for 27 years, ran a taxi service, and worked on projects for the Holiness Church and the town school. (Courtesy of the Mills County Soil and Water Conservation District.)

Everything west of the Pony Creek levee on the west side of Pacific Junction was under water in this view of the flood of 1952. The Missouri River finally crested at 27.3 feet before receding.

Sandwiches and coffee were served 24 hours a day at Rupe's in Pacific Junction during the flood of 1952. Behind the counter on the left stands Erma Lincoln while Joann Luddington pours coffee. (Courtesy of Richard Lincoln.)

Pres. Harry Truman is shown at the Burlington Railroad Depot in Pacific Junction in October 1952. Truman mocked a "Republican editorial" in the *Farm Journal* that claimed "the country has gone to the dogs," while another article in that issue questioned what farmers should do with their excess money. President Truman had previously appeared here in May 1950 on his 66th birthday.

Above is a threshing crew on the Benjamin Lincoln Farm in about 1900. Ben Lincoln later ran a butcher shop in Pacific Junction where he and his wife Margaret both retired to after they left the farm. Shown below is a corn harvesting scene on the Lincoln Farm west of Pacific Junction. (Both photographs courtesy of Richard Lincoln.)

Don Delashmutt Junior (left, in overalls) can be seen sandbagging with other gentlemen along a flooding Missouri River on June 16, 1967. (Courtesy of Richard Lincoln.)

Chickens and a cat find shelter on the Shirley Lincoln Farm northwest of Pacific Junction during a 1960 flood. George Fitch wrote in 1907 that the Missouri river made "farming as fascinating as gambling. You never know whether you are going to harvest corn or catfish." (Courtesy of Richard Lincoln.)

John Lincoln stands on top of the eroding levee at the Emory Kuhl Farm located on the east bank of the Missouri River across from the mouth of the Platte River during a 1960 flood. (Courtesy of Richard Lincoln.)

Shirley Lincoln is shown second from right in this line of tractors taken near Pacific Junction around 1954. During the 1930s, Lincoln began planting strains of hybrid seed acquired from Iowa State University, which led to the establishment of the Lincoln Seed Company that continued until 1959. (Courtesy of Richard Lincoln.)

Three

LYONS AND RAWLES TOWNSHIPS

By 1837, a Potawatomi village overseen by Chief Wabansi was established in the hills overlooking the Missouri River Valley. As the Potawatomi prepared to leave for Kansas, a group of Mormons established Rushville in 1846 on the west side of Keg Creek north of where it flowed into the Missouri River at the Five Barrel Islands. Frank Bullbona and other Potawatomi metis were their closest neighbors, but the disease-prone location was abandoned in 1848. The area later became known as Egypt, and a post office by that name operated in the 1860s during construction of the Council Bluffs and St. Joseph Railroad.

In 1852, Tabor was established in the hills to the east by John Todd and other migrants from Oberlin College in Ohio. However, Tabor remained outside the borders of Mills County until 1913, when the town annexed the neighborhood on the north side of the county line.

The Wahaghbonsy Post Office also opened in 1852. Two years later, the Wahayhbonsy Methodist Episcopalian Church was built on land given by William Wolfe. During the 1864 smallpox epidemic the church became a hospital where the sick were cared for by an old black man and a young girl. The church was then burned, and the present church was built in 1886. In 1892, the *Mills County Tribune* declared that the Potawatomi Chief's name was "spelled in more different ways than any other name in the state" with at least 37 different spellings of "Waughahbonsey."

In 1868, the Haney Station Post Office opened alongside the Council Bluffs and St. Joseph Railroad tracks near what is now Paddock Avenue east of 195th Street. In 1871, the Glenwood *Opinion* found 35 residents at Haney along with Young's Shoe and Boot Shop, Smith's Blacksmith Shop, and a dry goods and provision store operated by Thomas Morrow and Brother. In 1870, seventy-five train cars of corn, up to a thousand cords of wood, and a large number of cattle and hogs had been shipped from there by John Haynie and L. H. Gammon. There were 932 people in Lyons Township and 995 people to the east in Rawles Township according to the census of 1895.

This is a painting of Chief Wabonsi while on a visit to Washington, D.C., in 1835. He had earned his name during an attack on American supply boats on the Wabash River before the Battle of Tippecanoe. In 1837, the chief of the Potawatomi villages along the Kankakee River in Illinois helped move his people west to southwest Iowa but died before they moved on to Kansas.

These were the gullies along Waubonsie Creek in 1965. Wabonsi's village was situated where the creek intersected with its tributary, Shabonna Creek, near what is now Quandt Road and 235th Street. During the early 1870s, the Harmer and Brothers Woolen Mill was powered by the waters of Waubonsie Creek. (Courtesy of the Mills County Soil and Water Conservation District.)

The Wahaghbonsy Post Office is shown in the 1890s when it was home to the Kesterson family. Shown here, from left to right, are Emma, Alice, Sarah, Mary, Robert, and Charles Kesterson. The building was built in 1852 and closed as a post office 20 years later. It burned in 1924.

This was the home of Joseph and Eliza Wolf in the 1890s in Lyons Township. From left to right are Andrew Jackson Wolf, Charles Kesterson, Robert Kesterson, Mary Kesterson, Emma Wolf, Maude Wolf, Sarah Wolf, and M. Lafe Wolf. Joseph and Eliza Wolf are seated in front.

Center School in Rawles Township was situated alongside the stagecoach road that ran from Council Bluffs south through Glenwood and Tabor to St. Joseph, Missouri. In later years, much of this same route became U.S. Highway 275.

Site of the Shepardson Home

This was all that remained of the Shepardson home in the Elm Grove neighborhood of Lyons Township after the 1913 Easter Sunday tornado. Saloma Shepardson, her niece Alice Parsons, and her nephew Calvin Lambert fled to the cellar and survived uninjured, but embers from the stove burned the gutted house to the ground. The 1913 Easter Sunday tornado killed more than 150 people, most of them in nearby Omaha.

This was the Elm Grove School in Lyons Township in September 1934 with teacher Viola Kerns in the middle of the back row. Elm Grove first opened in 1857 and then moved in 1873. For a time in the early 1890s, a stage line ran from the Elm Grove neighborhood north to Mills Station halfway between Glenwood and Pacific Junction. The school was destroyed in the 1913 tornado and then rebuilt over the summer.

This is an early view inside the Elm Grove School when Dona Pritchard was the teacher. According to the note written on the back of the photograph, "My that old stove used to get hot."

This photograph was taken at Four Corners School in the early 1930s. Rachel (Swinney) Carlile is standing on the left, and her sister Pauline Swinney is on the right. Teacher Madeline Moses can be seen in the back. In the front row, second from right, is Roy Seeger, who was killed in action over Germany during World War II.

Transportation of Live Stock
by Truck Has Proven
Most Economical

Ruse Bros., Tabor, Ia.
Phone No. 8

Let your next shipment be by truck
Safer—Quicker—Cheaper

Ruse Brothers Trucking in Tabor was started by Oloney Ruse in the 1920s and continued until his death in 1975. The trucks hauled livestock to Omaha on the weekends and then grain during the week. Ruse also built the Ruse Super Service Station with his cousin and, in 1940, helped start the Tabor Feed Plant with Charles Adamson. (Courtesy of Wanda Ewalt.)

These are two views of the Tabor and Northern Railroad, which stretched all of 8.79 miles between Tabor and Malvern. The railroad originated with Dr. Thomas McClelland, the dean and professor of Philosophy at Tabor College, and began running in January 1890. The railroad made two trips a day, six days a week, along a circuitous route from Tabor to the wye in Malvern at Fourth Avenue and Second Street where the train could turn around. Operations came to an end in 1929 and the tracks and all equipment were sold at a sheriff's auction in 1934. (Both photographs courtesy of Rachel Carlile.)

These two photographs were taken on July 25, 1933, at the third annual Farmers and Merchants Picnic in Tabor. Activities included a parade, women's softball, baseball games, and more. The *Tabor Beacon* reported that 10 teams entered the "pulling contest" which was won by Paul Bell and his mules who hauled the sled carrying 4,100 pounds. Also, "Rombo the strong man," who was really an Evans from Rawles Township, allowed a "pneumatic tired tractor which was displayed on the grounds to run over his abdomen, and arose from the ground smiling after it had passed over."

Four

GLENWOOD TOWNSHIP

The Union Branch, Coonville, was organized in April 1848 by Mormon bishop Libbeus Coons, and the new community was mentioned in the Mormon *Frontier Guardian* that August. The town was surveyed in 1850 as Coonville then in 1853 as Glenwood, and the post office was renamed. In April 1853, Judge Bennett announced in the Mormon *Frontier Guardian* that lots were to be sold in Glenwood "in the heart of the richest agricultural and stock growing county on the Missouri slope, well supplied with timber, stone . . . best of springs, clean running brooks and excellent mill privilege." That year Lewis Johnson killed John Creech over a dollar bet on a 10¢-a-shot shooting match held near Walnut and Tyson Streets. Four years later, Johnson was tied together with his son and two other men and dumped in the Missouri River off the Platteville ferry.

Coonville's Traders Row along Locust Street was soon supplanted by the Plaza bounded by Walnut, First, Vine, and Sharp Streets. A brick courthouse was built at the center in 1857, but four years earlier it was "covered with brush," according to Daniel Solomon, and consisted of Peter Sarpy's trading post with William English as clerk, Townsend's General Store, and Luke Tinkle's Saloon. By 1860, there were almost 600 people in Glenwood, which grew to 719 white and nine "colored" residents in 1865.

In 1868, the Glenwood *Opinion* disparaged the "dangerous practice of shooting within town limits," but changes came fast after the Burlington Railroad was completed in November 1869. By 1870, Glenwood had over 2,000 people, and the Western Stage ran its last stagecoach west across Mile Hill Road to Pacific City. Local politics of the time were less than polite, and the *Mills County Tribune* reported that "old time Glenwood council meetings" often lasted until two in the morning. Much of the time was spent "cussing each other" with E. C. Bosbyshell representing Glenwood's "conservative element" and David Heinsheimer an "advocate of radical measures in all questions relative to the city's development." The population of Glenwood Township was 698 in 1895 with 2,143 people in Glenwood, including 24 "colored" residents.

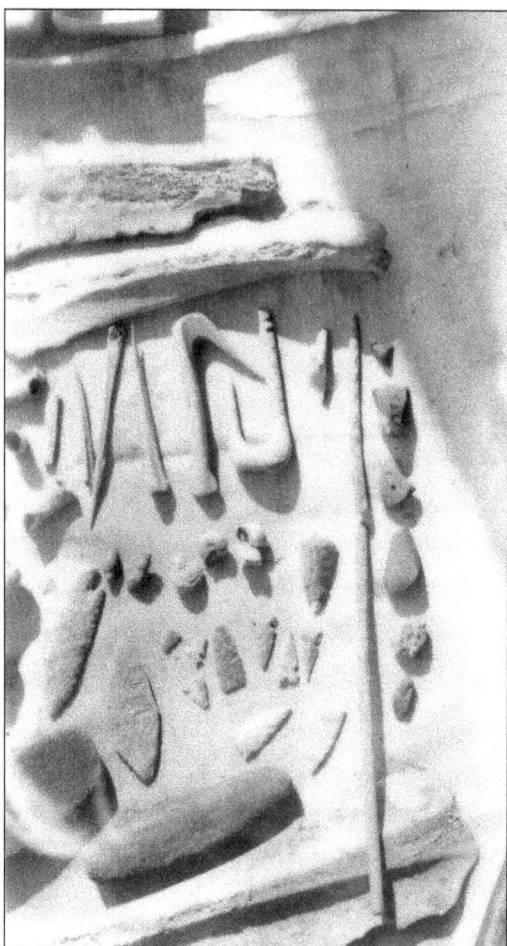

The artifacts at left were excavated in 1941 from the IIFMC, and the photograph below was taken by Ellison Orr during a 1938 excavation on the McManigal Farm north of Glenwood. Archeological sites dating from the Early Archaic have been discovered along Pony Creek and the Keg Creek Valleys, both of which became centers of the earth lodge horticulturists. By 1000 A.D., the people dubbed the Glenwood culture of the Nebraska Phase were raising corn, beans, sunflower, squash, pumpkin, and tobacco supplemented with wild game like buffalo and fish. Crop failures from severe and repeated droughts seem to have led to their abandoning the area by 1350.

John Hubbell is inside the buggy parked in front of what was then the Hubbell House Hotel at Locust and Coolidge Streets. The hotel was built in 1852 to serve the stagecoach line between St. Joseph, Missouri, and Kanesville, Iowa, with large stables in the back. A former stagecoach driver named George Painter ran the hotel in its early years, and it was later known as the Hudson House when it was razed in the 1920s. (Courtesy of the Glenwood Public Library.)

This was the northwest corner of Walnut and First Streets in the late 1860s. Barnabas Otis (shown in the top hat) constructed the building for his daughter Minnie Cole. It was torn down in 1922 to build a Standard Service Station.

This was the Mills County Courthouse at the center of the Glenwood Square from 1857 until the 1950s. It was built with the funds raised by county judge Oliver Tyson after he sold the county's swamp land. However, the State of Iowa had already deeded those same lands to fund construction of the Burlington Railroad west across Iowa. A swampland stink continued in the courts for years until an agreement was reached, and the Iowa Supreme Court awarded 10,000 disputed acres in Mills County to the railroad. The 1881 *History of the County* quietly noted that the "original legislation, the notices, the elections, the contract, all have disappeared from the county records for reasons best known to those immediately connected with their disappearance."

In 1866, the State of Iowa appointed a commission that included Glenwood attorney William Hale to locate the state's third Soldiers' Orphans' Home. Glenwood was selected after 15 acres were donated. By 1870, forty-one girls and fifty boys lived at the Soldiers' Orphans' Home in this three-story brick building. One orphan at Glenwood was future baseball player and evangelist Billy Sunday, and William Hale was later appointed governor of Wyoming Territory.

Glenwood's West Hill School, shown here, was built on Sharp Street in 1868. The building had six large schoolrooms, each with its own stove, along with recitation rooms. The school's caretaker was Maj. William English, who lived with his family in the basement. By 1878, there were 414 students at this school.

This was Sharp Street in Glenwood looking west toward Locust Street and the West Hill School in the early 1870s. During the 1860s, the Gilead Restaurant and Saloon at Sharp and Locust Streets promised "oysters, sardines, and hot coffee at all hours" in the *Glenwood Times* newspaper. Some of the businesses along Locust Street in the 1870s included Crow's Meat Market at Sharp and Locust Streets, Henry Yockey's Wagon Making and Repair Shop, and the Glenwood Iron Works and Foundry at Tyson and Locust Streets.

This was Sharp Street on the south side of Glenwood's Courthouse Square in the early 1870s. The businesses on the left include Charles Russell's Boot and Shoe Store adjacent to his brother Andrew's dry goods store and grocery. Some of the other businesses on the south side of the square listed in the Glenwood *Opinion* and the *Mills County Journal* include Eakin and Wicks Drug Store, Pettigrew and Company's "Cash House" General Store, I. and F. Heinsheimer's Clothing House, the Glenwood Harness Works, and the Dean and McCluskey City Drug Store seen on the right.

This was the Daniel Solomon home on Vine Street in Glenwood. Solomon was born in Virginia and graduated from Yale University in 1851. He arrived in Glenwood two years later and found work as the town's first public school teacher while he studied law. In 1857, Solomon was a delegate to the Iowa Constitutional Convention in Iowa City. He strongly promoted the Wabash Railroad through the county and helped establish the town of Solomon near his farm in Deer Creek Township. His home later became a boarding house called the Colonial Arms in the 1930s. It was razed in 2003.

The William Anderson home at Walnut and Second Streets was completed in 1870. Anderson was born in Virginia and came to Glenwood before the Civil War. He was partners with German immigrant Charles Staude in a general store on Walnut Street that also functioned as a private bank. In 1860, Anderson and Staude purchased the Missouri River ferry to Plattsmouth along with a new steam ferry called the *Paul Wilcox*. In 1871, Anderson and Joseph Hinchman founded the Mills County National Bank, and Anderson also was elected Glenwood city treasurer. Anderson died in 1891. His home later became the James mortuary and then apartments before it was razed in 2005.

This is an inside look at the D. L. Heinsheimer and Company Store on Sharp Street in 1888. The *Mills County Tribune* reported in 1891 that Heinsheimer's employed 15 to 20 clerks, used the "Lanson cash system," and specialized in "dry goods, clothing, hats, caps, boots and shoes, trunks, carpets, and wallpaper."

St. John's Episcopal Church was built in 1884 and originally stood at Second and Locust Streets. It is pictured here after 1890 when it was moved to its present location at Second and Vine Streets. The move was accomplished with the financial assistance of longtime member William Anderson.

The *Mills County Tribune* called this 1891 wreck on the Burlington Railroad line at Glenwood the "same old, old story with scarcely any variation" of the "foolish, oft tried experiment of two trains trying to pass on the same track at the same time, with the usual result." Six train cars were demolished, and the two engines were "jammed up pretty badly."

This was the front of the Ward Gunsolly and Company Grocery on Walnut Street during the late 1890s. The store's advertisement in an 1897 issue of the Glenwood *Opinion* promised, "Produce bought. Goods delivered."

The Soldier's Orphans' Home at Glenwood closed in 1876 and became the Iowa Asylum for Feeble-Minded Children, the seventh such facility in the country and the first west of the Mississippi River. By 1879, it was home to 200 residents with adequate room for only 140 of them. In 1882, the facility became the Iowa Institution for Feeble-Minded Children (IIFMC) and is shown here in the 1890s, when an electrical plant was constructed with six boilers and three engines to provide the institution its own light and power. The Glenwood *Opinion* noted that this necessitated "several miles" of wiring and 1,500 incandescent lights.

This was the view looking north on Walnut Street during the 1896 Glenwood Apple Carnival. Supt. Francis Powell of the IIFMC helped organize the event, served twice as president of the Iowa Horticultural Society, and owned two orchards outside Glenwood with 9,000 fruit trees.

The IIFMC Hospital was constructed in the 1890s and then expanded with an annex for tuberculosis patients, an X-ray laboratory, and offices for the institution's first dentist and psychologist. In 1912, the state began mandating sterilization for residents in places like the IIFMC, and from 1929 until 1974, the Iowa Board of Eugenics authorized the enforced sterilization of over 2,000 people, many of them solely because they had spent time at the institution in Glenwood.

This was a balloon ascension at First and Vine Streets in Glenwood in 1891. The *Mills County Tribune* reported that the balloon fell out of the sky like "some monstrous black witch that was coming down to spread terror among the inhabitants." Other activities that day included a wrestling match at the Armory, the "latest improved Edison musical phonograph" displayed at Heinsheimer's, and an exhibit of a two-headed baby, "a monstrosity from the western wilds of Nebraska."

This was how Lower Locust Street and Glenwood's Burlington Railroad Depot appeared in the 1890s. In 1879, a special train carrying former president U. S. Grant stopped here where he was greeted by an enthusiastic crowd, as were presidents Grover Cleveland in 1896 and William McKinley in 1898. In 1911, the *Mills County Tribune* reported on the funeral of "Commodore" Perry Stout, Glenwood's "aged colored fiddler" who had been born in slavery near Savannah, Missouri. Stout moved to Glenwood in 1865, and the funeral was held in his home on Lower Locust Street.

This 1890s view of Glenwood looks west at the orchards outside town as well as the large Glenwood Canning Company located on Locust Street south of Tyson Street. The cannery opened in 1882 and was reorganized in 1891 with David Heinsheimer as president. At times up to 150 people were employed to produce 30,000 cans of corn and tomatoes a day. Leroy Williams took over the business in 1897, when the cannery was awarded the contract to supply the U.S. Army's Department of the Platte with 5,000 cases of canned tomatoes.

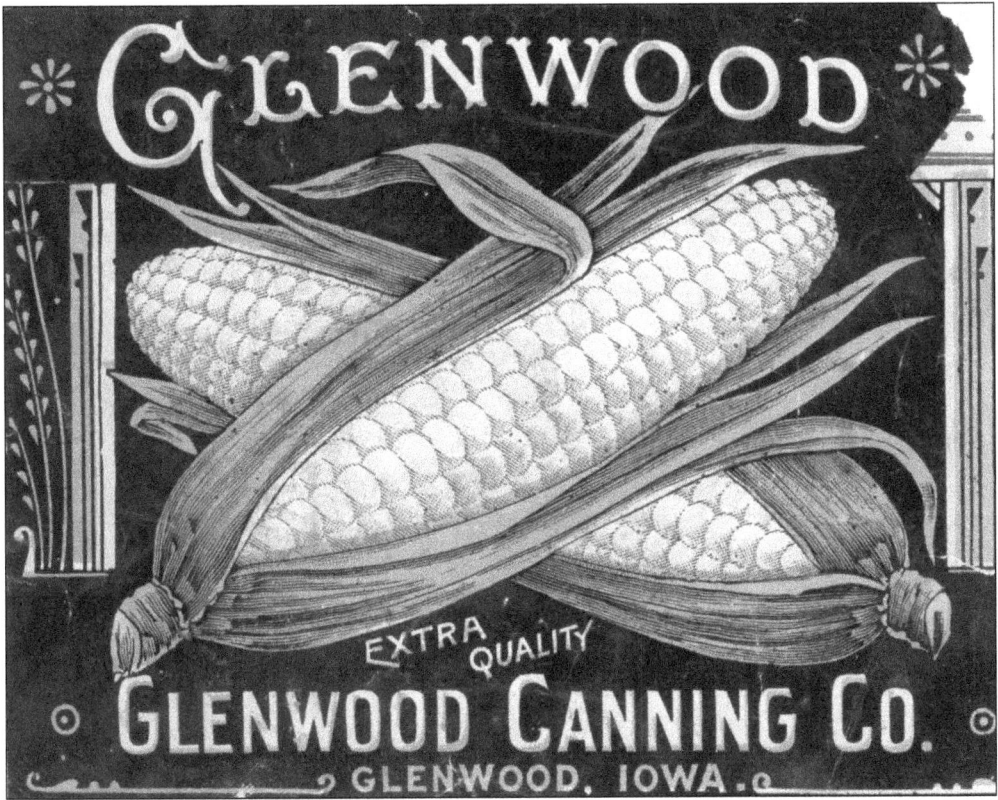

These labels are from the Glenwood Canning Company. In 1892, the cannery expected to contract 300 acres each of corn and tomatoes, and that decade operations were expanded with an evaporator, two large warehouses, and an office and scale on the south side of Tyson Street. Products sold under the brand name, The Glenwood, included canned tomatoes, sweet corn, beets, hominy, pumpkin, and baked beans. The cannery also produced up to 6 million of its own tin cans every year and was one the largest of the 17 canneries in Iowa by 1900. By 1907, only 4,000 cans were being produced daily and the cannery closed before 1914.

This view is looking northwest at downtown Glenwood during the 1890s. Businesses around the courthouse square included Ebaugh's Restaurant, the Commercial House Hotel, and the Buffington Bank on First Street. On Walnut Street were the Kiddoo Photo Parlor, John Carter's Meat Market, the Racket Store, the Gunsolly and Company Grocery, Stillwagon's Department Store, and M. G. Edwards Drug Store.

This was an apple tower at Sharp and Walnut Streets during one of the first Glenwood Apple Carnivals. During the 1890s, John Stone owned Iowa's largest orchard with 120,000 fruit trees on 800 acres west of Glenwood. In 1897, Stone's orchard had 11 varieties of apples and included 10 dwelling houses for seasonal laborers. Stone served as speaker in the Iowa House of Representatives, as a state senator, and two terms as Iowa Attorney General.

This was the Robinson Store at Sharp and Walnut Streets during the 1896 apple carnival. A native of Illinois, Lewis Robinson came to Glenwood in 1886 and found work at Ewing and Records' Book and Stationery Store. In 1889, Robinson took over the Glenwood *Opinion* and became the sole proprietor of the store two years later.

This was Glenwood's Burlington Railroad Depot decorated for an apple carnival. In September 1895, *The New York Times* reported "Low excursion rates brought in visitors by the thousands."

The buildings of the IIFMC stand on the hill overlooking Sharp Street on the south side of Glenwood's Courthouse Square during the 1890s. In 1897, the IIFMC included an experimental orchard with 200 varieties of apples developed by Supt. Francis Powell, who served as superintendent from 1882 until 1904.

Wagons and buggies make their way along Walnut Street with goods piled high on the wooden sidewalks in this 1890s photograph. The last remaining two-story, wood-frame building on the west side of Glenwood's Courthouse Square was built in 1856 by Milton Martin and was occupied by R. H. Daniel's Hardware when it was replaced with a new brick building in 1905.

This is a look inside Matthew McCluskey's Drug Store on Sharp Street. McCluskey built a new building four years after the 1888 fire. D. G. Jamison and Company's General Store was originally in the eastern section of the building but expanded into the drugstore by 1918. This was later the location of Shehan's Department Store and then LaRue's Pharmacy from 1976 until 2006.

The McCluskey family is shown from left to right in 1899 with Floyd and John standing and William, Jennie, and Matthew seated. Matt McCluskey was a Civil War veteran who came to Glenwood in 1870. The McCluskey home at Second and Vine Streets in Glenwood is now the Raynor-Hertz Funeral Home.

Unloading potatoes at Louis Hurst Bldg   East side 11

This photograph shows Louis Hurst's on Vine Street on the east side of Glenwood's Courthouse Square. Hurst was one of Glenwood's Jewish merchants and had specialized in a little bit of everything since he came to town in 1890, including produce, scrap metal, secondhand goods, and junk.

This is a photograph of a baptism in the murky waters of Keg Creek that took place in Glenwood in 1898.

This photograph shows a Grand Army of the Republic meeting at the Mills County Courthouse around 1910. This organization of Union veterans was an important, and vocal, political constituency in Iowa during the late 19th century.

This was the Farm Cottage at the IIFMC in 1904. During the early 20th century, the farmland at the institution included an orchard, greenhouse, herd of swine, and dairy. A new dairy built at the IIFMC in the 1930s was the first in Iowa with modern milking facilities. (Courtesy of Rachel Carlile.)

The Glenwood Granite Works is shown around 1895 when its operations were confined to a one-story building on Sharp Street. Fred Starbuck is seated on a monument, and Milton Richards is shown sitting on the sidewalk. In 1895, the *Mills County Tribune* reported that Starbuck offered a "fine line of granite and marble monuments," and in 1901, over 69,000 pounds of marble were shipped from Vermont to the granite works. This building is now the Sharp Street Tavern.

This was the Hubbells' home in Glenwood at Locust and Coolidge Streets with a bridge in front to cross the Locust Street ditch. J. R. Hubbell died here at home in 1926. (Courtesy of the Glenwood Public Library.)

These are two views of the Glenwood Lake Park around 1910. The park originated in 1907 after the Burlington Railroad deeded their former right-of-way along what is now Lake Drive. The Mills County Historical Museum at the park was organized in 1957 and grew to include the machinery hall in 1967 and a Burlington Railroad car and the Cottington Barn in the 1980s. The Davies Amphitheater opened at the park in 1981. (Both photographs courtesy of Gary Roenfeld.)

The Glenwood Board of Trade is shown around 1900. Second from left in the second row is David Heinsheimer, who had helped establish the organization in 1891 to bring electric lights and a waterworks system to Glenwood. Heinsheimer also served on the Glenwood City Council, was elected mayor, served many terms on the Glenwood school board, and was president of the Iowa State Bankers' Association when he died in 1914.

This was the intersection of Sharp and Walnut Streets around 1911. That autumn the *Mills County Tribune* reported that an "Army of apple pickers and packers" had invaded town. Five apple-packing plants were then in operation with Jonathan apples bringing $2 to $3 a barrel, picked and delivered. (Courtesy of Gary Roenfeld.)

The Cheyney Meat Market on First Street was operated by Robert Cheyney and his four sons Jack, Charles, Harry, and Paris. Robert and his wife, Mary, had come to Glenwood from Pennsylvania in 1883, and he retired from the business around 1900. The Cheyney Brothers Meat Market closed in 1945, and the building later housed the Gaylord's I.G.A. Market and Burdick's I.G.A. Market.

Participants in an International Order of Odd Fellows (IOOF) convention are lined up along First Street in 1904. The town's IOOF Lodge 97 was first organized in 1856, and membership included some of the town's most successful businessmen. In early 1894, the Odd Fellows hosted a dance to celebrate the opening of their hall on the second floor of the new Glenwood Opera House, which has been known as the Rex Theater since 1922.

The offices of the *Mills County Tribune* are shown in 1914, when the newspaper was housed in Tunis Records' Midway Building on Sharp Street. The *Tribune* first appeared in 1891 after Nelson Field took over the *Mills County Journal*. Wayne Choate purchased the *Tribune* in 1927 and merged it with its longtime competitor, the Glenwood *Opinion*. In late 1998, the rear portion of the Midway Building collapsed, and the building was razed. (Courtesy of Rachel Carlile.)

The Glenwood Public Library on Vine Street was built in 1907 after IIFMC Superintendent Powell arranged a $7,000 donation from Andrew Carnegie. The library was organized by the Glenwood Women's Club in 1896 and was originally on the second floor of the Racket Store on Walnut Street.

William Jennings Bryan, three-time Democratic candidate for president, is shown here fourth from left during an appearance at a Glenwood Chautauqua around 1907. Second from left is lawyer Louis Genung, who supported Bryan as an Iowa delegate to the 1900 National Democratic Convention. Between Genung and Bryan stands Albert Heinsheimer, and on the far right is Professor Maus, superintendent of Glenwood schools.

The IIFMC boys' custodial building was completed by 1908, which allowed 150 more people to be admitted. In 1908, the population of the IIFMC reached 1,100 people overseen by a staff of only 175. The next year the Iowa legislature increased the appropriation to $12 annually per resident. English immigrant Dr. George Mogridge was appointed superintendent in 1903.

The Glenwood Community Band is shown in 1920 when Ed Schuloff was bandleader. One notable member was Mayo Buckner, who was placed at the IIFMC by his mother in 1898. Buckner could play the trombone, baritone, violin, cornet, clarinet, and cello; directed the choir; scored music for the institution's orchestra; and had an I.Q. of 120. His obituary appeared in *Time* magazine in October 1965 after he died at the age of 75.

The Glenwood First Congregational Church on Second Street was organized in 1856 by John Todd and seven others. Construction of the church started in 1857, and in the early years, the basement was leased as a pork packinghouse during the winter to help fund construction.

This postcard shows apples being loaded on Burlington Railroad boxcars at Glenwood. In October 1891, the *Mills County Tribune* reported that over 4,000 barrels of apples had been shipped out of Glenwood the previous week with 12,000 barrels shipped that season. Ridgeway's Glenwood Cooper Factory reportedly produced almost 100,000 barrels that year.

This is a group of Glenwood apple pickers around 1909. George Pitsenberger is shown on the far left with Guy Pitsenberger third from left. Second from right is Harvey T. Rimel, Mills County's first casualty during World War I.

The United Methodist Church in Glenwood was first organized in 1853. In 1876, a large brick Methodist Episcopal church was constructed just south of the older church. That church was sold in 1905 and remodeled into what became the Dean Hotel. The present Grace United Methodist Church, shown here, was built at Second and Walnut Streets in 1905, with an adjacent brick parsonage constructed in 1939.

1715   New Grace M. E. Church, F.M.C. Glenwood, Ia,   Pub by L.S. Robinson.

The Glenwood Post Office at Vine and Sharp Streets was built in 1919 at a cost of $55,000. At the time, the Glenwood postmaster was W. F. Fickel. Fickel had left Ohio with his family in 1873, and his father died of smallpox just two weeks after they arrived in Mills County. Fickel was elected Mills County Treasurer in 1906 and moved to Glenwood, where he served as postmaster from 1913 until 1921. In 2003, the Glenwood Post Office was renamed in honor of the late Iowa congressman William Scherle.

The Glenwood Armory was built on Walnut Street just south of the Glenwood House Hotel in 1914. Company I of the Iowa Third Infantry was based here and was sent to the Mexican border in 1916. They left for France in May 1918 during World War I and returned home in 1919 as part of the "Red Bull" Division. That summer the veterans organized American Legion Post 141 in honor of Harvey T. Rimel. The building later housed Glenwood City Hall, the police station, and the fire department until it was razed in 1975.

Glenwood's Third Ward schoolhouse was built at Third and Chestnut Streets in 1886. This was the former location of Western Iowa College, which then became a Methodist seminary until 1878, when it was purchased at a sheriff's auction by the Glenwood school board.

These are two interior views of the L. S. Robinson Store, one of Glenwood's longest running family businesses. Lewis Robinson Sr. sold the Glenwood *Opinion* in 1920 and retired from the store in 1932. The business was then operated by his son Lewis Robinson Jr., who served as chief of the Glenwood Fire Department for many years. He sold it to his son Lewis Robinson III in 1969. The view below was taken on June 1, 1929, and shows Lewis Robinson Sr., Mildred Hatcher, and Lewis Robinson Jr. inside the store from left to right.

In late 1891, the Glenwood Electric Light and Power Company was organized with Matt McCluskey as president. Four months later, this powerhouse was built on First Street between Locust and Walnut Streets.

Edd Marshall's funeral rigs are shown lined up out front of his Blue Front Livery on Sharp Street in June 1915 before Charles Rathke's funeral. Marshall had purchased the livery from his father in 1910 and built a new building on Sharp Street in 1928 to open a Pontiac and Oakland automobile dealership.

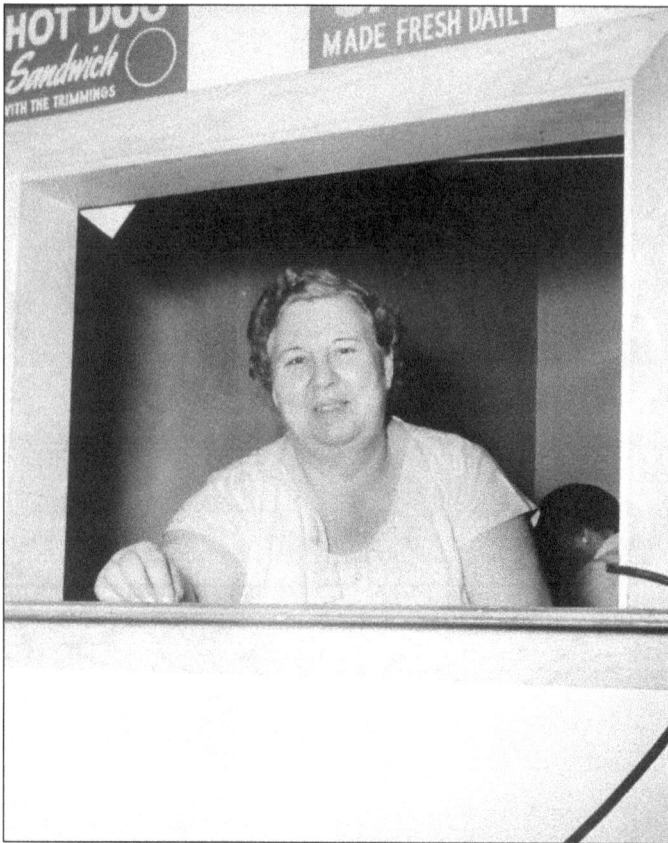

Edna Rodman is shown behind the counter of her restaurant, Edna's Café, in the early 1960s. She graduated from Glenwood High School in 1931 and had helped her mother and sisters cook for the Rotarians and the general public. Edna married Lewis Rodman Jr., operated her café in downtown Glenwood, and raised three children on the family's farm north of Glenwood.

Ervin Ling stands next to a patrol car during the 1940s in front of the Mills County Jail on Vine Street. The jail was built in 1915, and Sheriff Elisha Bushnell died while inspecting the construction when he fell from the scaffolding.

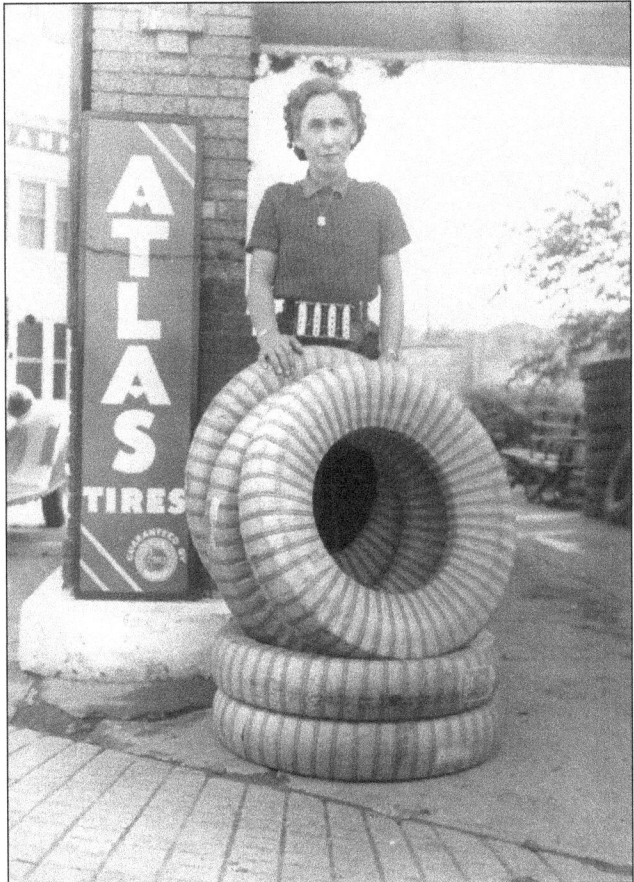

Case's Standard Service Station at Walnut and First Streets was built in 1923 and was long remembered for the pine tree that grew through its roof. Luther Case took over the station, which was operated by his daughter Abbie (shown at right) from 1933 until 1983. The gas station and adjacent Estes Hotel were demolished in 1995 and replaced by an expanded parking lot for Glenwood State Bank. (Both photographs courtesy of Jeremy Rodman.)

Dec. 1937

This was Sharp Street on the north side of the Glenwood Square on December 18, 1937. The *Opinion-Tribune* newspaper reported that Santa Claus came to town in an airplane piloted by "Glenwood aviatrix" Dorothy Broadfield. He arrived on the square in a fire truck with "candy for all the kiddies," and local merchants gave away holiday gift baskets.

The Glenwood Lodge 58 of the Ancient Free and Accepted Masons was organized in 1855. The Masonic Lodge acquired the First Baptist Church at First and Vine Streets in 1915, which was rebuilt in 1922 into the Masonic Temple shown here. This building was razed in 1975 and replaced with a smaller building that is now the Glenwood Senior Center.

An inside view of Daniel's Hardware on Walnut Street is shown above. Robert Daniel came to Glenwood in 1866 and worked as a deputy sheriff before he went into the hardware business. He later bought out the lumber company at First and Locust Streets. After Robert's death, his sons William and Homer took over the business and opened Glenwood's Ford automobile dealership shown below on First Street, where the first V-8 Ford in the county was displayed in 1932. The hardware business was sold to Paul Records in 1947 and closed in 1959.

This photograph shows the IIFMC juvenile cottage. The facility had been renamed the Glenwood State Hospital-School by 1957, when the grounds were opened to the public for the dedication of the V. J. Meyer school building. The institution population peaked at Glenwood in the early 1960s with over 2,000 residents before changes were implemented to provide more community-styled settings. The former IIFMC is now the Glenwood Resource Center and home to over 300 residents.

The Glenwood High School was built in 1937 on the site of the West Hill School. Over $57,000 in federal funds were used to complete the building, which was designed by the architectural firm of Keffer and Jones. This later became Glenwood Junior High, the Glenwood Middle School, and, presently, West Elementary. (Courtesy of Gary Roenfeld.)

Roth Packing opened in Glenwood in 1946. During the early 1950s, 1,400 cattle a week were slaughtered at what the *Opinion-Tribune* called the "largest Kosher beef house in America." The packinghouse workers shown here in 1952 are, from left to right, (first row) Dwight Myers, Dean McKay, Sam Lee, Jim Keager, Dean McDelroy, and Calvin Detlef; (second row) Jake Taenzler, Darrel Wilson, Ray Danley, Wade Huff, Earl Barber, Ervin Kay, and Joy Bartles. The packinghouse later became Glenwood Packing until it closed in 1965. It was re-opened by Swift and Company two years later and employed 255 people when it closed in August 1985.

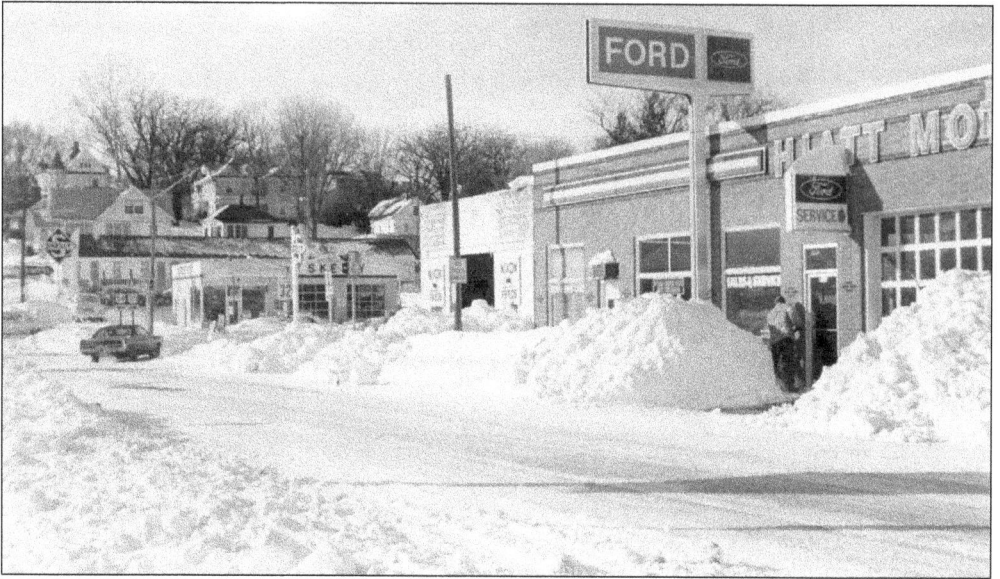

This photograph shows Hiatt Motors in January 1971 after two blizzards swept through with 50-mile-per-hour winds. Hiatt Motors was located in the 1928 Edd Marshall building on Sharp Street. Glenwood's Ford automobile dealership later became Bill Nissen's Ford and was Hawkins-Marsh when it closed in the early 21st century.

The burning-the-mortage celebration of the American Legion building at Vine and First Streets is shown here in January 1986. Seated at the table, from left to right, are Ron and Ruth Hurst, Vera Tackett, John Dean, Charles Tackett, and Ruth Hamm. Those burning the mortgage, from left to right, are Charles Hunt, Don Langholz, Don Burwell, and Evan Miller. (Courtesy of Genevieve Hunt.)

Five

CENTER TOWNSHIP

The Fayette Post Office opened in 1856 near modern-day Ives Avenue and 270th Street and was followed by Mount Olive Post Office in the 1860s. The summer after the Burlington Railroad built through, the Glenwood *Opinion* reported that "Flagtown alias Stringtown alias Fayette alias Loudon alias Mount Olive, has been aliased again and now sails under the beautiful title of Hillsdale." Hill's "general mercantile business" was open along with McEvans's grain elevator and Hillsdale was surveyed that year. In 1874, Hillsdale grain dealer and English immigrant James Mickelwait was elected to the Iowa legislature on the "anti-monopoly ticket," and the Hillsdale Methodist Church was dedicated.

A tax passed in 1875 created the Mills County Poor Farm on 210 acres purchased from Jesse Miller. Center Township appeared in 1879 following a petition signed by Jacob Shoemaker, T. M. Britt, and 180 others. Superintendent Smalley had 15 residents at the county poor farm in 1880, and a Hillsdale fire burned the grain elevator, depot, and hotel. Hillsdale was incorporated the next year with prohibitionist Isaac Kelley, the first mayor, and during the 1880s, Hillsdale included the Chambers Hotel, Andrews Dry Goods, Staggs Grocery, Thomas Dry Goods and Grocery, two doctors, a wagon shop, and a one-room jail. A stagecoach ran to Tabor, and in 1883, the telephone line was strung from Glenwood. By 1889, the community had the *Herald* newspaper, stockyards, Mickelwait and Coates's 15,000 bushel grain elevator, a baseball diamond and horse track, meat market, and normal array of small town businesses.

There were 746 residents in the township in 1895 with 211 residents of Hillsdale. Then the Burlington Railroad surveyed a new line that opened in 1904, and the first news from Balfour appeared in the Malvern newspaper soon afterwards. The Hillsdale grain elevator burned again in 1904 with a thousand bushels inside, and the *Opinion* reported it would be rebuilt at the "new station . . . three miles north." The Balfour Post Office opened in 1905 inside Aaron Burson's store, and the Hillsdale Post Office closed in 1909. The Balfour Post Office closed in 1927. The poor farm and its cemetery were sold in the 1950s to construct the current Mills County Courthouse.

This was the Silver Number Two school in 1920, located west of where the Wabash Railroad crossed Silver Creek. Shown here, from left to right, are students (third row) Alfred Kruse, Madge Moses, Teddy Kruse, Katie Hamann, teacher Myrl Holiday, and two unidentified; (second row) Geneva Richardson, Harry Kruse, Marvel Moses, Helen Gilbert, Irene Brooks, unidentified, and Phyllis Holiday; and (first row) Elaine Gilbert. The school closed in the early 1940s.

The Pleasant Grove School in Center Township stood near what is now the intersection of U.S. Highway 34 and 270th Street.

This was the Burlington Railroad Depot at Hillsdale. The town's first depot burned during an 1880 fire, which also destroyed the nearby two-story hotel and store operated by Isaac Kelley, along with the Mickelwait and Coats grain elevator with 7,000 bushels inside.

This was the Hillsdale School in 1896, located at Mills and Second Streets. There were 142 students registered in 1881, although the daily attendance was often only half that number. The school remained long after the town had dissipated and was destroyed in a fire during the 1930s. It was replaced by a smaller structure that remained in use until school consolidation in the early 1960s.

Sitting in front of this home in Hillsdale is Wesley Hutchison with his daughter Ollie Hutchison Winger and granddaughter Hazel Winger Deacon. After the Burlington Railroad moved its tracks north, Ollie Winger and her husband Samuel moved to Balfour where she took in laundry.

The Hawthorne School in Center Township was built during the first decade of the 20th century near what is now Lambert Avenue and 225th Street. It was closed in the early 1960s, and the school building was moved a mile north and converted into a residence.

This was a store at Balfour in 1911, seven years after the Burlington Railroad relocated its main line east of Glenwood. C. N. Schultz and Aaron Burson both opened stores at Balfour. A. B. Judson moved the two-story IOOF building north from Hillsdale to house a general store in Balfour with upstairs meeting rooms for the Silver Grange 1702 of the Patrons of Husbandry.

My third year in school. Florence Linville is the teacher

This was the Barbee School northwest of Balfour in 1928, when Florence Linville was the teacher. Posing for a class picture, from left to right, are (third row) Emil Roenfeldt, Ollie Jens, Bernard Roenfeldt, teacher Florence Linville, and Alta Jens; (second row) Elva Stacy, Ellen Jens, Genevieve Jens, Olive Stacy, Emma Stacy, Darlene Jens, and Violet Stacy; and (first row) Wilmer Jens, Leonard Jens, Alfred Stacy, Leon Chambers, and Edward Jens. (Courtesy of Genevieve Hunt.)

Six

INGRAHAM TOWNSHIP

Ingraham Township was first created through a petition led by Daniel Goodwin to divide Silver Creek in 1855. During that decade, the Ward Tavern opened to serve the stagecoach line between Council Bluffs and Des Moines, and a post office opened briefly in the late 1860s. In 1870, German immigrant George Pullman came by wagon to the 160 acres of prairie land in the township that he'd bought for $10 an acre.

The construction of the Council Bluffs and St. Louis Railroad through the Henry Harrison Huffaker Farm spurred the appearance of Silver City. Over the summer of 1879, A. W. Crosby opened the first store in town, which was soon followed by Moore's Drug Store and Wiatt's General Merchandise. The town was platted by the railroad company that fall, and in November 1879, the *Mills County Republican* newspaper reported that Silver City was filled with "Men running this way and that way. Some with spades and others with lumber on their shoulders."

The town was incorporated in 1883, and in 1891, the *Mills County Tribune* noted that the town boasted "four doctors, two drug stores, three ministers of the Gospel, and Jackson and Elliot own a hearse." During the 1890s, the Silver City Driving Park Association operated a half-mile horse race track, complete with grandstand. The *Tribune* also noted that Ingraham Township was home to George Rew, the county's "heaviest cattle feeder" who ran 900 head of cattle on 2,200 acres along with almost 100 horses, a "good sized drove of hogs," and "enough cribs, barns, sheds, etc. . . . to make a small sized village." In 1895, there were 731 people in Ingraham Township, with 407 residents of Silver City.

This was G. A. Spelbring's Concert Orchestra based in Silver City. The band was made up of eight violinists, two clarinets, four horns, cellist C. E. Wilson, C. E. Boyer on trombone, three saxophonists, pianist Margeret Spelbring, drummer Fern Spelbring, and June Fickel as vocal soloist. (Courtesy of Brenda Bichel Lewis.)

This was a 1950 photograph taken by Violet Roenfeld looking north at the east side of Main Street in Silver City. In 1882, everything along this side of the street burned to the ground, except for the Hintz Hotel and the Russell General Store. Eleven buildings on this side of the street burned down again in 1891 after a fire started in Pullman and Hettingers General Store.

This was the Silver City School in 1950. The town's first school opened in the fall of 1880. The second school opened in 1895 on the hill overlooking town along present-day May Street, with additions built in 1911 and 1926.

These Silver City schoolchildren are shown in April 1932 with Drexel Decker third from right in the back row. The last class of nine students graduated from Silver City High School in 1961.

This Silver City lumberyard is shown here in 1950. A man named Bateman opened a lumberyard at an early date, which was then sold to Greenwood lumber.

This is a 1950 photograph of the grain elevator in Silver City. Edwin Moore built the first grain elevator at Silver City in December 1880 with a capacity of 25,000 bushels. The elevator at Silver City is now owned by Farmservice Company.

The Silver City Jail was constructed in 1911 when Miles Huffaker was mayor. The first tenant was a transient named Miller who was discovered asleep in a boxcar wearing the millinery items that were being shipped to Clara Plumb of Silver City.

This was the Donald Goos Farm north and east of Silver City in July 1975. The terraces had been constructed on the farm during the previous year. (Courtesy of the Mills County Soil and Water Conservation District.)

Seven

SILVER CREEK TOWNSHIP

In 1847, Alpheus Cutler established Cutler's Camp along Silver Creek in what was known as the Big Grove at Rock Ford Crossing. Cutler was formerly a high-ranking Mormon official who grew disenchanted with Brigham Young and later established his own branch of the Mormon Church at Manti near Shenandoah. The small community on Silver Creek had several cabins and a general store, and during the 1850s, it included a sawmill and the large Rock Ford gristmill built by Aaron Lewis.

The 1869 construction of the Burlington Railroad across Mills County prompted John Paddock to build a house and open a dry goods store with his brother. A post office appeared in January 1870 originally called Milton Station, likely after the English poet, and J. D. Ladd built a grain elevator. In March 1870, the Glenwood *Opinion* called the Paddock brothers the "pioneers of this place," which also offered a "good boarding and eating house" with "one smith shop and one saloon." By July, the new town had 60 houses, three dry good stores, two groceries, the Curtis House and Malvern Hotels, and other businesses.

Milton Station officially became Malvern by 1871, and the community was incorporated the next year. Reverend Roe opened the Baptist Centennial Academy in 1875, which later became the Western Iowa Normal School. Due to an illegality, Malvern was reincorporated in 1878, and Silver Creek Township was redefined in 1880 to exclude anything inside Malvern city limits.

The Council Bluffs and St. Louis Railroad was built diagonally across the township and through Malvern in 1879, and the Tabor and Northern Railroad was constructed north into Malvern in 1890. In 1891, Malvern hosted the county's first suffragist convention where feminist Carrie Chapman Catt spoke twice. During the early 1890s, the *Mills County Tribune* complained that cattle were "allowed to run at large" in Malvern, which "should not be tolerated," and also reported on a "special train" of students from Tabor College who came to Malvern over the Tabor and Northern Railroad to attend the "colored folks' fandango" at the Malvern Opera House.

In 1895, there were 1,091 people in Malvern and another 460 residents of Silver Creek Township.

The East Liberty Church was built in 1875 east of the site of Cutler's Camp. The Jewell Post Office was opened near here in the 1870s, and the neighborhood located along present-day Hutchings Avenue west of 310th Street was later known as Wall Street. The Rock Ford mill on Silver Creek, built in 1856, was operated for many years by George Patrick and was torn down in 1912.

The Center Line School was north of Malvern and across the road from the Center Line Fruit Farm and the Axtell's Orchard Hill Farm. The road in front of the country school is now U.S. Highway 34, which stretches from suburban Chicago west through Rocky Mountain National Park in Colorado.

This was the Burlington depot at Malvern on Main Street north of Eleventh Street after the railroad moved its line to the north side of town. Previously, the Burlington depot was located near Fifth Avenue and Third Street near the stockyards and the Wilkinson and Coats grain elevator.

The Wabash Railroad depot in Malvern stood on the south side of Fifth Street between Third and Fourth Avenues.

93

This was part of the late 19th century tangle of railroad tracks on the south side of Malvern where the Wabash, Burlington, and Tabor and Northern Railroads all converged.

The Malvern Roller Mills on the right stood at Second Avenue and Second Street near the grain elevator and the town's original Burlington Railroad Depot. The original Malvern mills were built by Brothers and McIntosh in 1875, a mile to the south in the Peaceville neighborhood.

This was First Avenue in Malvern looking north in 1900. At the time, Malvern had a population of around 1,300 people with two newspapers, the *Leader* and the *South West Iowan*, and four hotels, the City Hotel, the Cottage Hotel, the Garman Hotel, and the Gordon House. Other businesses included the Chicago Dry Goods Company, J. L. Buckingham's Billiard Parlor, wagon maker James Brohard, the Retelsdorf Brothers Restaurant, and blacksmith Ulysses Graves.

This was the automobile show at the 1912 Mills County Fair. The first county fairs were held in Glenwood until 1873, when the Mills County Central Agricultural and Mechanical Association was organized as a joint-stock company. The new association purchased the grounds south of Malvern where the fair has been held annually except in the years 1898, 1934, and 1935.

This is Malvern looking east across Boehner Pond from Malvern Cold Storage. The pond provided ice for the business, which opened in 1882 as a pork packinghouse. Over 10,000 hogs were slaughtered before it closed in 1886 and was later converted into a temperature controlled storage facility by Bennett, Thorne and Company of Philadelphia. A. B. Hawkins and Leonard Boehner took over in 1895, when the facility had a capacity of 40,000 barrels of fruit. The focus later shifted to ice manufacture, a creamery, and extensive chicken and egg processing with products sold under the brand name Nishna. After World War II, the plant was leased to Blue Star to supply troop rations. In 1957, the Malvern egg plant was in operation 24 hours a day, six or seven days a week, with 145 employees. It was later sold to Continent Egg, and a portion was leased to produce dried eggs for Henningson Foods until 1982.

The Presbyterian Church Malvern started in 1872. At first, the congregation alternated Sundays to share a church with the Baptists until 1874 and then the Methodists until their own church was finished in 1876. In 1979, the Presbyterian congregation at Malvern joined with the town's Methodist congregation.

This was the Malvern freshman high school class of 1922. At the start of the 21st century, the Malvern School District merged with Nishna Valley to form the East Mills School District.

Mr. Horstmeyer and his team is shown by the Burlington Railroad tracks in Malvern.

This is an aerial view of Malvern during the late 1940s. Notice the fairgrounds near the bottom of the picture with Malvern Cold Storage and Boehner Pond to the left on the west edge of town. (Courtesy of the Mills County Soil and Water Conservation District.)

Eight

INDIAN CREEK TOWNSHIP

In 1854, Julia Hoyt began teaching school in her cabin in the North Grove neighborhood in Section 20, and Herman and Sarah Abel came down from Canada to settle in Mills County. Accordingly, the Indian Creek Post Office was opened in Section 28 from 1854 until 1859. The township was created in 1857 when it was still wide-open prairie, and that May the Glenwood *Opinion* reported that the seven-year-old daughter of Mr. Rockafellow had died in a fire while the family was out burning stubble in the fields.

The Burlington Railroad was built through in 1869, which quickly led to the establishment of Emerson and Hastings. Life was still hard for some though, and William David recalled the June 1875 invasion of "the Kansas grasshoppers," which "flew so thick they darkened the sun" and devoured the crops. David lost his job as a farmhand south of Hastings and, by that fall, found work husking corn "from daylight until dark to get fifty bushels, for which we were paid two cents a bushel." By 1895, there were 601 people in Indian Creek Township, with 501 people in Emerson and 366 in Hastings.

This shows the Burlington Railroad's depot at Emerson in 1908 above and in 1911 below. The community was named after Ralph Waldo Emerson, and Lewis Tubbs moved to town as a land agent for the railroad. In July 1870, the Glenwood *Opinion* noted that Emerson "started but a few weeks ago, has ten buildings, five of which are business houses," including a dry goods store, a grocery/provision house, lumberyard, and a corn buyer/commission merchant. Baptist minister Eber Loomer held the town's first religious services in the Burlington Railroad Depot the next month. By 1880, Emerson had a population of 400 people.

The Greenwood Lumber Company was on the corner of Howland and Bradford Streets in Emerson. Standing in front is Charles Davis Greenwood, who is one of the five children of C. G. Greenwood and his wife Mary, who came from Maine to Mills County to start a lumber business with yards at Silver City, Emerson, Imogene, and Treynor. C. G. Greenwood served in the Iowa legislature, as did his grandson Roscoe Greenwood.

Emerson's first school was paid on subscription and taught by William Rice. After he left for Yankton in Dakota Territory, the town's first school building was built in 1873. This photograph shows the Emerson public school constructed in 1898 between Manchester and Howland Streets.

This was the Emerson home of Marion Evans. In 1877, Marion herded a thousand head of cattle from St. Paul, Minnesota, south to Mills County using two dogs and a team of horses hauling a buckboard wagon. In 1883, Marion married Judge Tubbs's daughter Hattie, and their youngest son Kenneth went on to serve as lieutenant governor of Iowa from 1945 until 1951.

Street Scene, Emerson, Iowa.

This was Emerson around 1900 looking east on Morton Avenue from Manchester Street. At the time, Emerson had a population of around 500 people and the weekly *Chronicle* newspaper. The *Chronicle* appeared in Emerson in 1876 when fourteen-year-old Fred Boehner moved the newspaper from Malvern and ran it for the next three years.

Cattle crowd the streets of Emerson as they are driven to the stockyards along the Burlington Railroad tracks near South Avenue and Bartlett Street. Emerson livestock dealers listed in the 1903 *Polk's Iowa Gazetteer* included Charles Bruen, Elihu and Horace Cheney, George Cross, Albert McClain, C. C. Oakes, and George Warner.

The Burlington Railroad Bridge across Indian Creek at Emerson looked like this in 1912. In June 1982, the Amtrak California Zephyr derailed twice at Emerson due to flooding along Indian Creek. Mayor Jack Evans sent out requests across the globe asking for donations after the town was turned down for disaster assistance by the federal government.

The Emerson Opera House was built in 1891 on the corner of Manchester Street and Bradford Avenue, which later became the location of city hall.

This shows Emerson in 1930 when U.S. Highway 34 was being paved from Hastings east through Montgomery County along the Blue Grass Route of the 1920s. In 1934, U.S. Highway 59 was created, which now runs from Manitoba south to Laredo, Texas, and passes through the east side of Emerson as Crawford Street.

This is an aerial view of the Otha D. Wearin Farm in Indian Creek Township. Josiah Coe Wearin passed through on his way from Indiana to California in 1850. He then returned to Indiana and, in 1854, brought his wife Olive and two of their children to the prairies along the West Nishnabotna River. They were soon joined by Josiah's sister Experience, his father Michael, and his brothers Otha, Andrew, and Harry. (Courtesy of the Mills County Soil and Water Conservation District.)

This is a photograph of Otha Donner Wearin, who was born on his family's farm outside of Hastings. His reports on European farming were printed by Iowa newspapers, and he was first elected to the Iowa legislature at the age of 25. He married Lola Brazelton in 1931, and the next year was elected the youngest member of the New Deal Congress. He served in the House of Representatives until 1938. Wearin was the author of several books, was elected to the Cowboy Hall of Fame, and died in Glenwood in 1990. (Courtesy of the Otha D. Wearin family.)

This 1932 photograph shows Otha D. Wearin campaigning on the east side of Indian Avenue in Hastings. Some of the businesses in town that decade included Colling's General Store, the Cox Grocery, Priest's Drug Store, and the Van Arsdall Shoe Repair. (Courtesy of the Otha D. Wearin family.)

The Burlington Railroad Depot at Hastings was on the north side of the railroad tracks at Tarkio Avenue. The town was platted in 1870 on what the Glenwood *Opinion* called a "handsome plateau" just south of where Indian Creek entered the West Nishnabotna River. C. W. Brandon opened the town's first business, and a post office opened in 1872. The *Plaindealer* newspaper appeared in 1879 to promote the Greenback political party.

This is a view of Hastings looking southeast during the 1880s. Some of the businesses then included the Applegate Grocery, Goodell's General Store, the McDonald and Noonan Saloons, and Sheffer and Bulla's Hardware Store. J. A. Parrish manufactured the Little Giant Windmill, and barbed-wire fencing was produced by Alvin Sherman. (Courtesy of the Otha D. Wearin family.)

This photograph shows the hotel in Hastings that was located at Tarkio Avenue and South Railway Street south across the tracks from the Burlington Railroad depot. It was Perry's Hotel when this photograph was taken in about 1889 and was also known as the Foster's House and the Hastings Hotel. (Courtesy of the Otha D. Wearin family.)

This was the inside of the Hastings Post Office around 1900. The postmaster at Hastings during the Cleveland administration was Clinton Genung, the oldest son of Louis and Julia Genung. Louis Genung was a Civil War veteran who served time in the Cahaba prison in Alabama during the war. He got married in Illinois in 1865, headed west to Nebraska and the Rocky Mountains, and then moved to Mills County where he remarried in 1872. (Courtesy of the Otha D. Wearin family.)

Harry Keffer is seen here behind the counter of George Keffer's Hardware in Hastings around 1910. (Courtesy of the Otha D. Wearin family.)

The Hastings Methodist Episcopal Church is shown here around 1910. The congregation first organized in 1870, and a church was built in 1889 using stone quarried near Henderson with lumber donated by A. J. Wearin and Charles Donner. The church was enlarged in 1920 and visited by Dr. Norman Vincent Peale in 1979 after the congregation won an award from his *Guidepost* magazine. (Courtesy of the Otha D. Wearin family.)

The west side of Indian Avenue in Hastings is shown here around 1909. One longtime Hastings merchant was Civil War veteran James Martin, who came to Indian Creek Township in 1873. Three years later, he started working for E. P. Bosbyshell in Hastings. Martin took over the store in 1893, and by 1901, the store advertised in the *Mills County Tribune* that it was the "largest and best equipped dry-goods establishment" in the eastern half of the county. (Courtesy of the Otha D. Wearin family.)

This was the grain elevator, water tank, and depot along the north side of the Burlington Railroad tracks at Hastings in 1910. At that time, the stockyards were located just west and north of the elevator, which was then owned by J. R. Graham with a capacity of 8,000 bushels. (Courtesy of the Otha D. Wearin family.)

This was the Burlington Railroad's coal chutes at Hastings, which was also the terminus of the Nebraska City, Sidney, and Northeastern Railroad branch built southwest to Sidney, Iowa, in 1878. Two years later, the Burlington branch known as the Hastings and Avoca Railroad was built north to Carson, Iowa, where it connected with the Rock Island Railroad. (Courtesy of the Otha D. Wearin family.)

This is the West Nishnabotna River at Hastings. One of the many ways to spell the name of the river was provided in 1785 by Esteban Miro, the Spanish governor over Louisiana and Florida. He called it the Nichenanbatone. It was the Nis-na-botona to Brackenridge in 1811, the Nisinibotany to John Dunbar in 1835, and in 1842, Henry Carleton called it the Nishnebottona. (Courtesy of the Otha D. Wearin family.)

This was the Hastings High School class during the 1890s. Seated in front on the left is teacher and principal Adaline Birdsall who came to Hastings in 1892 and later married J. F. Martin, the president of the school board.

This shows the inside of the grammar room at the Hastings School. The town's first school was built in 1876, burned down in 1891, and was then rebuilt in 1893. It was torn down in 1964. Student Iva Ord is shown in the center of this photograph.

This was the Nishna Valley School in 1974. The school district was formed in 1960 after the consolidation of the schools in Emerson, Hastings, Henderson, and Strahan, and this building was dedicated in 1963. In the first decade of the 21st century, Nishna Valley was consolidated with the Malvern School District and became known as East Mills.

Nine

White Cloud and Deer Creek Townships

White Cloud started as a ferry crossing on the West Nishnabotna River in the early 1850s and was named after suggestions ranging "from Sour-Mash to Zionville" were rejected, according to W. H. Taft. The Underground Railroad went through White Cloud, including a family of four and one young man, all escaped slaves, who passed through in July 1854. Two years later, a post office was opened, and White Cloud Township was organized through the petition of Sam Johnson, Harvey Summers, and others.

The completion of the Burlington Railroad proved to be the end of White Cloud, as its residents and even business buildings were moved closer to the tracks. In later years, Lawrence was on the east bank of the West Nishnabota River where the Council Bluffs and St. Louis Railroad crossed the Burlington Railroad branch to Sidney. Most people still called it White Cloud, and during the 1890s, there was a section house, a water tank, and Salyers and Kayton's grain elevator. The Burlington Railroad branch to Sidney also created Clark, which was surveyed in 1879, and a post office opened. The post office closed four years later, and Clark was vacated by 1889.

The town of Strahan appeared in 1880 after the Council Bluffs and St. Louis Railroad was completed and was named after Malvern businessman James Strahan, a Hoosier who had headed west with the California Gold Rush. Strahan businesses in 1882 included W. F. Hannah and Company, which offered clothing, dry goods, groceries, and implements, and Kayton and Kinney, grain dealers with a grocery. The Strahan Post Office was housed inside Ron Kier's Grocery when it closed in 1955, and the store closed in 1969.

The eastern portion of White Cloud became Deer Creek Township. A United Brethren congregation was organized in 1855, the South Grove cemetery appeared the next year, and the Turner Post Office opened during the 1870s. Glenwood lawyer Daniel Solomon's 640-acre "model farm" in Deer Creek was described by the Glenwood *Opinion* as having 13 miles of Osage Orange hedge fencing with "orchards, stable lot, feed lot, vineyard, stockyard" connected by 60-foot wide lanes.

The town of Solomon appeared in 1880 in Section 33 of Deer Creek Township, and a post office was open until 1900. By 1895 there were 627 people in White Cloud Township and 689 in Deer Creek Township.

The White Cloud Mill on the West Nishnabotna River is shown here in the early 20th century. Henry Hamaker opened his first mill at White Cloud in 1853 and then built a covered toll bridge across the river. In 1867, the Glenwood *Opinion* noted the "old shanty situated diagonally to the points of the compass" that offered "Council Bluffs beer" at White Cloud and, the next year, listed S. T. Brothers' General Store and the Star Dry Goods "at the sign of the red flag."

This was the west side of the White Cloud Mill in November 1937 shortly before it was torn down. This mill was built in 1879 with a capacity of 50 barrels of flour a day that were sold under the names White Cloud Chief and Hamaker's Best. During the 1880s, mill operations were taken over by Henry and Eleanor Hamaker's son, George Hamaker, who operated the mill until about 1906.

This was the Strahan Consolidated School in 1974. In 1917, Strahan started the county's first consolidated school, which was built the next year south of the town. It opened in September 1918 with 168 students, and boys' and girls' basketball teams were organized the next month. The first high school class graduated in 1921, and the last class of eight students graduated from Strahan High School in 1960. The building then housed elementary students until 1971 and was razed in the early 1980s.

The Strahan United Methodist Church was dedicated in 1884 and then destroyed by a tornado two years later. It was rebuilt in 1886 and then remodeled in 1929 with a basement, furnace, and other improvements. The church still stands alongside what is now 360th Street, north of Paddock Avenue.

This photograph shows the West Nishnabotna River as it flows through White Cloud Township. From its headwaters in Carroll County, the West Nishnabotna River runs south and southwest through Crawford, Pottawattamie, and Mills Counties before it meets the East Nishnabotna River near Riverton, Iowa, and then empties into the Missouri River near Watson, Missouri. (Courtesy of the Mills County Soil and Water Conservation District.)

This photograph shows the Union Country School in Deer Creek Township, which was located near what is now Queen Avenue and U.S. Highway 59.

This is Ellen Dolph at her family's homestead at South Grove in Deer Creek Township in the 1970s. She was the fourth generation of her family on this farm, which was settled by Aaron Dolph in 1849. The Dolph farm home shown here was built in 1884. Below is a photograph taken by Ellen Dolph of her fields in July 1979. She died in 2009.

This photograph shows Katie Robbins of Solomon, which was surveyed on the Wabash Railroad line in 1880.

The Glynn School was located just north of Solomon in Deer Creek Township along the east side of what is now 390th Street, north of Rains Avenue.

Mrs. Max Shook, a Hastings farm wife, shown above, was the only woman competitor in the third annual Midwest Plow Terracing Contest. The contest was held in September 1944 on the Charles Kayton Farm south of Strahan with 15 competitors from seven southwest Iowa counties. Lynn Stevens of Malvern (shown below) was the winner. (Both photographs courtesy of the Mills County Soil and Water Conservation District.)

Ten

ANDERSON TOWNSHIP

In the early 1850s, a settlement of Mormons appeared along Farm Creek, a tributary of the West Nishnabotna River, where they established a branch of the Reorganized Church of Jesus Christ of Latter Day Saints (RLDS) and started a cemetery in 1852. The next year the area east of the West Nishnabotna River became Montgomery Township. This later became Mud Creek Township and then Union Township before acquiring its present name. The Big Mud neighborhood also had its start in the 1850s with a school that later became Benton, when a post office was opened in 1863. H. S. Woodmansee had a dry goods and grocery store at Benton by 1868, and the Big Mud Church was built in 1873 and was later known as the Wesley Chapel.

The Benton Post Office closed in 1881 after the completion of the Burlington Railroad's Hastings and Avoca branch that ran along the east bank of the West Nishnabotna River, north to Carson. The new railroad led to the establishment of Potter, which was platted in April 1880 as Henderson Crossing, and the first train passed through three months later. Some of the new town's early businesses included William Creamer's General Store and Bone and Plumb's Hardware.

Henderson was incorporated in 1893 and by 1895 had 255 residents with 855 people living in Anderson Township. Henderson provided an important outlet to farmers in northeastern Mills County, and the *Mills County Tribune* noted in 1913 that 229 train cars of livestock and 85 train cars of grain had been shipped out.

The Pickerill School in Anderson Township was located just east of the tracks of the Burlington Railroad branch between Hastings and Carson. The site of the school would be along modern-day Ellington Avenue around 390th Street.

The first Box Elder School in Anderson Township opened in 1874 near what is now Brothers Avenue and 340th street. The school, and neighborhood, was named after the tributary of Mud Creek. The Box Elder Post Office was open during the 1890s northwest of the school. The last teacher at Box Elder was Ferne Stewart, who earned $250 a month when the school closed in 1960.

C. B. & Q. DEPOT & ELEVATOR HENDERSON IOWA. BY GRAVES NO 2

This was the Burlington Railroad Depot and the grain elevator in Henderson. The original portion of the town was laid out on the east side of the railroad tracks. In 1880, Swedish immigrant Peter Asell was named section foreman at Henderson. The railroad line north to Carson was abandoned in 1972, and the town's post office closed in 2008.

The Farmer's National Bank in Henderson is shown here in 1904. In 1930, the bank was robbed during a daylight holdup by three men who fled town with $927. The bank closed its doors later that decade.

This photograph of the Henderson flour mill was taken from the town's grain elevator. The mill was built in 1915 by W. H. Harbor, was powered by electricity, and produced 25 barrels of Flavo flour a day.

The Henderson Consolidated School's bus fleet is shown here in 1923, when the buses were built in town by Wilson Truck Manufacturing. A vehicle a week could be turned out by George Wilson and his handful of employees. The one and a half ton GWWs, named for George W. Wilson, were designed to deal with southwest Iowa's mucky roads, and about 300 trucks and school buses were produced until ill health forced Wilson to close down in 1932.

After a 1925 fire caused severe damage in Henderson, the community established its own volunteer fire department. George Wilson was the first fire chief, and his company also built the town's first fire truck, seen here.

The grand entry into the Henderson Rodeo was led by Darrell Smith (left) and Don Smith (right) in this photograph from the early 1960s. The annual event started in 1938 to raise funds to purchase the community a new fire truck and continued until 1978.

This was the Henderson School, constructed in 1908, that became Henderson Consolidated in 1920. The last class of ten students graduated from Henderson in 1960, and the school was used for elementary classes until 1971. The building was razed in 1980.

This was the Henderson Methodist Church that was constructed in 1906. In 1882, Joel and Sarah Woods had deeded the land for a church for a dollar and then donated the money back.

Rogene Holt Parker is shown at the Henderson switchboard. Henderson's first telephone service was started in 1900 by Joe Sell. The town switchboard was originally in the Carse Building until the early 1940s, when it was moved next to the Citizens' Bank. In addition to operator, Parker also did the company's books until 1961, when the switchboard closed following the introduction of direct-dial telephones.

Visit us at
arcadiapublishing.com

www.ingramcontent.com/pod-product-compliance
Lightning Source LLC
Chambersburg PA
CBHW050657110426

42813CB00007B/2036